FOCUS I:

John Sloan

The Wake of the Ferry, II

Exhibition organized and text
written by Grant Holcomb

Timken Art Gallery • San Diego
October 2–December 2, 1984

This exhibition has been made possible, in part, by a
grant from the John Sloan Memorial Foundation, Inc.

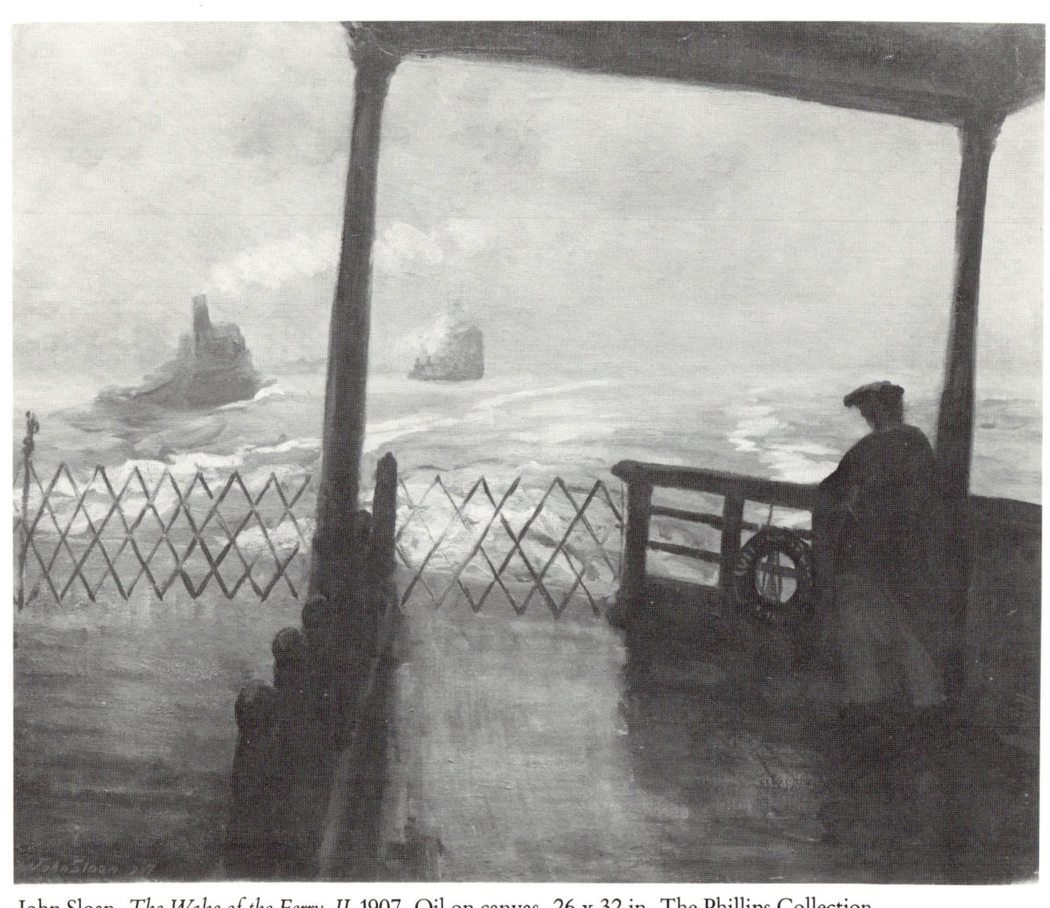

John Sloan. *The Wake of the Ferry, II*, 1907. Oil on canvas, 26 x 32 in. The Phillips Collection.

ISBN 0-9610866-2-9

Foreword

"FOCUS I: John Sloan, *The Wake of the Ferry, II*" is the first in a series of exhibitions designed to enhance our understanding of a single major work of art and to meet the challenge put forth by critic James Johnson Sweeney: "One fine painting thoroughly appreciated, like one great book well read, would have more cultural effect than a world of digests or surveys."

The majority of the Focus exhibitions will be curated by guest-scholars and will explore the history and significance of paintings in the permanent collection of the Timken Art Gallery. Occasionally, they will introduce us to major paintings in other collections. In this respect, we are indebted to Mr. Laughlin Phillips, Director, and Mr. Willem de Looper, Curator, of The Phillips Collection in Washington, D.C. for allowing us to borrow one of the key examples of early twentieth-century American painting, John Sloan's *The Wake of the Ferry, II*.

In organizing the first Focus exhibition, we have had to rely on the talent and support of many people. First and foremost is Helen Farr Sloan whose encouragement and generosity over the years have been crucial. To her, and to the John Sloan Memorial Foundation, Inc., our deepest thanks for helping make this exhibition possible. Other individuals who provided valuable assistance whenever needed include Nancy Andrews (San Diego Museum of Art); Joseph Bellows (Museum of Photographic Arts, San Diego); William I. Homer (University of Delaware); Alan H. Jutzi (The Huntington Library); Eric S. McCready (Archer M. Huntington Art Gallery, University of Texas at Austin); Arthur Ollman (Museum of Photographic Arts, San Diego); John A. Petersen (Timken Art Gallery); Richard R. Reilly (James S. Copley Library, La Jolla); Lewis I. Sharp (The Metropolitan Museum of Art) Stephen and Mus White (Stephen White Gallery, Beverly Hills); and Judith Zilczer (Hirshhorn Museum and Sculpture Garden, Smithsonian Institution).

We are also grateful for the cooperation of the lenders to the exhibition: Hirshhorn Museum and Sculpture Garden, Smithsonian Institution, Washington, D.C.; The Archer M. Huntington Art Gallery, the University of Texas at Austin; Memphis Brooks Museum of Art, Memphis, Tennessee; Milwaukee Art Museum, Milwaukee, Wisconsin; The

Metropolitan Museum of Art, New York, New York; The
Phillips Collection, Washington, D.C.; and the Stephen White
Gallery, Beverly Hills, California.

The publication of the catalogue could not have been
accomplished without the ready assistance of Mary Farris who
helped organize and design the catalogue; Sally Yard who
offered sound advice and criticism; Nancy Emerson who helped
with the numerous administrative details; and Mary Holcomb
who helped evaluate the many versions of the manuscript. To
these four, our many thanks.

Finally, as the Focus exhibitions represent a new direction
for the Timken Art Gallery, we would like to express our
gratitude to the gallery's Board of Trustees, under the direction
of Mr. Allen J. Sutherland, and Nancy Ames Petersen, Director
of the Timken Art Gallery, for their encouragement and
support of this project.

Grant Holcomb
Associate Director
Timken Art Gallery

John Sloan
The Wake Of The Ferry, II

John Sloan (1871-1951) has long been regarded the pre-eminent painter of the Ash-Can School, that group of American artists who observed and painted the miscellany of city life during the first decades of the twentieth century.[1] Vilified by critics as "The Apostles of Ugliness" and the "Revolutionary Black Gang," these artists embraced the ordinary acts of everyday life and celebrated the burgeoning spectacle of urban America:

> Here, before their eyes, was the untouched panorama of life, an unlimited field, an art bonanza. Here is the Alligator Cafe and the Bowery, the Haymarket on Sixth Avenue, the ferry-boats, the lower East Side, in any number of cheap red-ink restaurants, one found subjects as undefiled by good taste or etiquette or behavior — that national hypocrisy — as a new-born babe.[2]

This interest in the pictorial significance of the city directly challenged the prevailing "good taste" embodied in academic canons of art that demanded inoffensive subject matter, technical proficiency, and conformity to acceptable classical traditions. Sloan and the city realists rejected this genteel tradition and turned to the colorful, at times sordid, aspects of daily life for the same reason that Huckleberry Finn left the Widow Douglas — "everything's so awful regular a body can't stand it."

The apparent commonness of *Three A.M.* (Fig. 1), for example, shocked the academicians. An ordinary moment in the lives of two working women was considered inappropriate subject matter. Such a theme possessed little moral value and had little, if any, picturesque beauty. Furthermore, the muted palette and vigorous brushwork countered the Academy's preference for overly sweet color and emphasis on drawing. Finally, objections might be directed at the standing figure scantily attired in a nightgown. (It should be remembered that four of Sloan's etchings of New York city life were declared too vulgar for public exhibition in 1906). Though Sloan sent *Three A.M.* to the jury of the National Academy of Design for possible exhibition in 1910, he admitted sending it "as much as a joke, like slipping a pair of men's drawers into an old maid's laundry . . . ."[3]

Milton Brown aptly summed up this new attitude in American art:

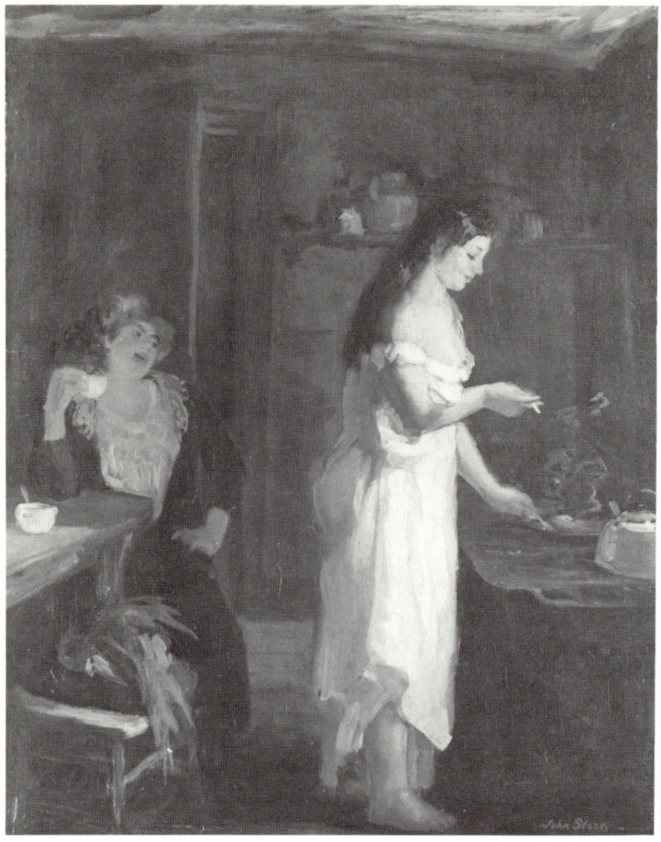

In a sense this was a revolt against genteel vision, which sought an ideal and pleasant existence totally removed from the harshness of industrial reality, and the substitution for it of a democratic insistence upon the varied and particular aspects of the normal daily existence of the masses of people.[4]

An academic predilection for taste, decorum, and propriety fell before a Whitmanic onslaught of "the sunburnt, the unshaven, the huge paws."[5]

Sloan's genre paintings of New York City have come to epitomize the work of the Ash-Can School. Yet his interest in contemporary urban life appears to have developed in Philadelphia a full fifteen years prior to his moving to New York. We know, for example, that Sloan purchased a copy of John Collier's book *A Manual of Oil Painting* in 1889. Collier provided the young artist with technical information on the art of painting and addressed the issue of appropriate subject matter: "For many reasons modern subjects ought to be best. After all, *what is going on around us at the present day is more interesting . . . than all the records of the buried past*" (italics

Fig. 1 John Sloan. *Three A.M.,* 1909. Oil on canvas, 32 x 26 in. Philadelphia Museum of Art; Gift of Mrs. Cyrus McCormick.

mine).[6] In 1893, Sloan's close friend, Robert Henri, gave him a copy of *Modern Painting* by George Moore. We again approach a fundamental source of Sloan's philosophy of art when we read:

> The great artist is he who is most racy of his native soil
> . . . . Character is everything in art . . . . A national
> character can only be acquired by remaining at home and
> saturating ourselves in the spirit of the land until it oozes
> from our pens and pencils in every slightest work, in
> every slightest touch.[7]

Certainly Sloan and Henri discussed thoroughly and responded favorably to the ideas put forth by Collier and Moore. Indeed, Henri's well-known article on the 1910 Exhibition of Independent Artists specifically recalls these early sources:

> As I see it, there is only one reason for the development
> of art in America, and that is that the people of America
> learn the means of expressing themselves in their own
> time and in their own land . . . . What we . . . need is
> art that expresses the *spirit* of the people of today.[8]

Sloan began painting the drama of Philadelphia city life during the nineties. By 1901, he had announced to the press that he was "at work upon a series of studies of city scenes," being "a believer in the capabilities of the modern American city for artistic work."[9] It is commonly agreed, however, that Sloan did not find himself as an artist until he moved to New York City in 1904:

> In every way the move to New York was a turning
> point. It meant giving up newspaper work on a
> salary, the substitution of free-lance magazine
> illustration, and his increasing commitment to creative
> work as a painter and etcher.[10]

Sloan was an indefatigable observer of the city and, with the poet Walt Whitman, could exclaim "all hours of the day and night bring to me copious pictures."[11] Rarely did he have to travel far to find suitable motifs to paint. His many walks through the streets of the city brought him into direct contact with the varied currents of daily life. Ambling down Fifth Avenue, Sloan found himself "on the edge of a wind storm, the air full of dust and a sort of panicky terror in all the living things in sight."[12] The following day he began to paint, from memory, *Dust-Storm, Fifth Avenue* (The Metropolitan Museum of Art). While walking to Henri's studio, he observed "a humorous sight of interest. A window, low second story, bleached blond hair dresser bleaching the hair of a client. A small interested crowd about."[13] He soon began painting, again from memory, *Hairdresser's Window* (Wadsworth Atheneum). Sloan enjoyed immensely this parade of humanity. "It is all the world," he declared, "Work, play, love, sorrow, vanity, the schoolgirl, the old mother, the thief, the truant, the harlot. I see them all . . . without disguise."[14] The city pictures of New

York fully reveal the beauty Sloan found in the daily life around him. His people romp on the beaches, gaze longingly into shop windows, frolic in the public squares, and delight in the new invention called "the movies." The paintings possess what John Butler Yeats termed "a sense of the perennial charm of humanity."[15]

It is true that Sloan was the historian of New York, the pictorial chronicler par excellence of life on the streets and in the public squares. Yet he was also keenly aware that the rivers surrounding Manhattan held the city in their grip and subtly influenced and enhanced the lives of the urban dweller. As we shall see, it was the artist (the painters, poets, and photographers) who, at the turn of the century, preserved the true sense of the rivers at a time when they were being polluted by raw sewage and oil burning vessels.

The American experience has been inextricably linked to the sea as Roger Stein and John Wilmerding have demonstrated in their illuminating studies of marine painting in American art.[16] The boat is an image commonly found in American marine painting and, with the sea, became a central figure in many of the literary and artistic masterpieces of the nineteenth century. The genius of American literature can be traced in the voyages of the "Pequod," the raft of Huckleberry Finn, and the Fulton Street ferry that took Walt Whitman between Brooklyn and Manhattan. Equally significant images of the boat appeared in American painting of the time: William Sidney Mount's *Eel Spearing;* George Caleb Bingham's *Fur Trappers Descending the Missouri;* Winslow Homer's *Eight Bells;* Thomas Eakins' *Max Schmidt in a Single Scull;* and Albert Pinkham Ryder's *Toilers of the Sea.* All denote the seminal role that the boat played in the development of an artistic genius in America.

John Sloan's 1907 painting *The Wake of the Ferry, II* continued this grand nineteenth-century tradition and remains one of the best-known images of the boat/river motif in American painting. Furthermore, it sustained the belief that the ferryboat was one of the most poetic elements of city life. As Lewis Mumford recently noted in his autobiography, the ferryboat's "change of pace and place, from swift to slow, from land to water, had a specially stimulating effect upon the mind" and, as he concluded, they were worth running "if only to give sustenance to poets and lovers and lonely young people . . . ."[17] And it was a poet who boldly introduced the ferryboat into our cultural heritage.

Walt Whitman recorded the following passage in his 1849 notebook: "Many works have been written, to describe journeys between the Old and New World, and what was done or seen therein, and afterward. But we know of no work . . . describing a voyage across the Fulton Ferry."[18] Seven years later Whitman wrote the renowned poem "Crossing Brooklyn Ferry."

The ferryboat ride from Brooklyn to Manhattan was one of the poet's primary diversions. "Crossing Brooklyn Ferry" reveals Whitman's love for both cities, the waters surrounding them, and the crowds of men and women who returned home on the ferry each day. His descriptions of the familiar sights and sounds of city and water became symbols of the eternal cycle of life in this poem of passage. Though the poem was largely ignored when it was published,[19] Whitman's interest in the unpoetic moment and his ability to find beauty in the commonplace had far-reaching consequences for the arts in America.

In many ways, William Dean Howells' response to the New York scene anticipated the paintings of the Ash-Can School and often his writings suggest specific paintings by Sloan.[20] Percy Bysshe Shelly Ray, the protagonist in *The World of Chance,* rides the ferry and, leaning over the railing, absorbs the bustling activity of the city. Recalling Sloan's figure in *The Wake of the Ferry,* Ray gazes upon the shoreline and reflects on "the beauty struggling through the grotesqueness of the huge panorama, and evoking itself somehow, from the grossest details."[21]

William Carlos Williams, a contemporary of the city realist painters, brought the Whitmanic vision into twentieth-century poetry. In his 1914 poem, "The Wanderer," we again see the poet "crossing the ferry / With the great towers of Manhattan before me, / Out at the prow with the sea wind blowing."[22] Williams uses the image of the ferryboat crossing in order to explore and answer the question "How shall I be a mirror to this modernity?" The poet accepts the rawness and vulgarity of the city and, like the city realist painters, finds an "old man who goes about / gathering dog-lime" more majestic and more astonishing than the prosperous and the proud.[23]

Many of America's finest writers captured the color and mood of the city's rivers at this time. In addition to Howells and Williams, the names of Stephen Crane, Theodore Dreiser, and Edna St. Vincent Millay also come to mind. Millay's poem "Recuerdo," for example, continued the poetic delight in traveling on the foredeck of the ferryboat and, in its straight-forwardness and use of realistic details, appealed to artists who explored this theme of crossing by water.

The visual artists were equally responsive to the rivers that encircled Manhattan. Like their literary counterparts, they rejected the genteel tradition and used the river and the

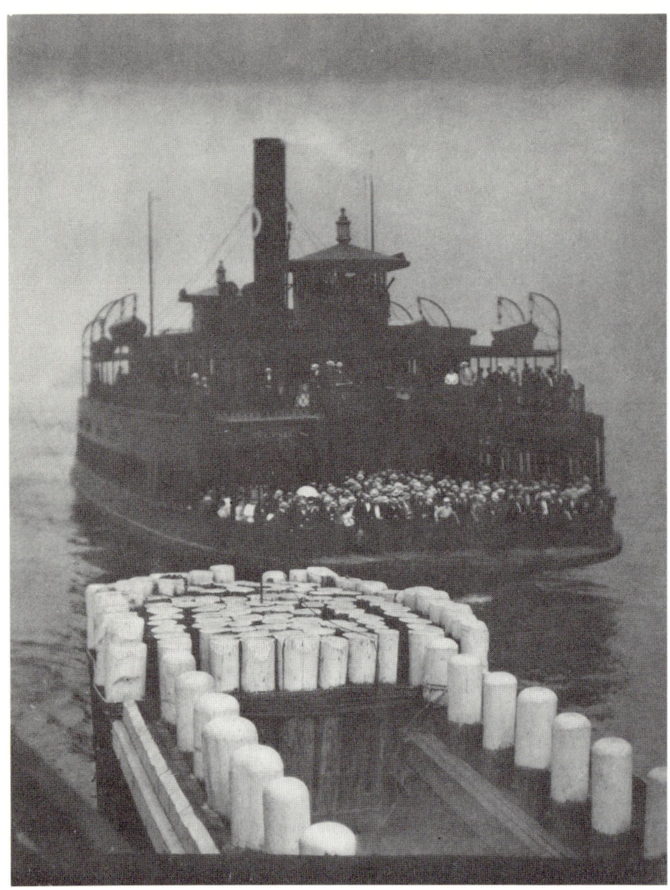

ferryboat in order to identify with the ordinary reality of city life. Alfred Stieglitz, the founder of the Photo-Secession[24] and one of the pioneers of modernism in America, responded to the events of daily life and was a sensitive observer of the human drama:

> Wherever I looked there was a picture that moved me —
> the derelicts, the secondhand clothing shops, the rag
> pickers, the tattered and the torn. All found a warm spot
> in my heart. I felt that the people nearby, in spite of their
> poverty, were better off than I was . . . . There was a
> reality about them lacking in the artificial world . . . [25]

This is Whitman's world of the "sudorous and sweaty classes."[26] Furthermore, Stieglitz's comments and choice of subject matter, as well as the dates of the photographs themselves, raise the question of his relationship to the Ash-Can School. One critic felt that Stieglitz's influence on the city realist painters was direct and immediate:

> His [Stieglitz's] *Winter-Fifth Avenue*, made in 1893,
> created a sensation not only in photographic circles, but

Fig. 2 Alfred Stieglitz. *The Ferry Boat,* 1910. Photogravure, 8⅛ x 6½ in. The Stephen White Gallery, Beverly Hills, California.

in the world of art, and blazed the way for a whole school of painters, who set themselves the task of depicting the streets and life of New York.[27]

And though Stieglitz scholar William I. Homer had stated that "it is hard to detail whether Stieglitz influenced the painters or vice versa . . . ,"[28] his recent research concluded that "Stieglitz's realistic treatment of urban subjects seems to presage the painter's imagery."[29] Certainly, *The Ferry Boat* (Fig. 2), a 1910 photogravure, depicts a familiar sight: a ferryboat (the earliest form of mass transportation in New York) filled with daily commuters. The picture's aesthetic significance is derived from the harmonious relationship of tones, the simplification and repetition of forms, and the abstractness of design. The subdued tonal effects and the formal simplicity reflect the influence of James A. McNeill Whistler, the ex-patriate artist whose "nocturnes" and "symphonies" excited an entire generation of American painters and photographers.

Stieglitz admired the early cityscapes of Karl Struss, a

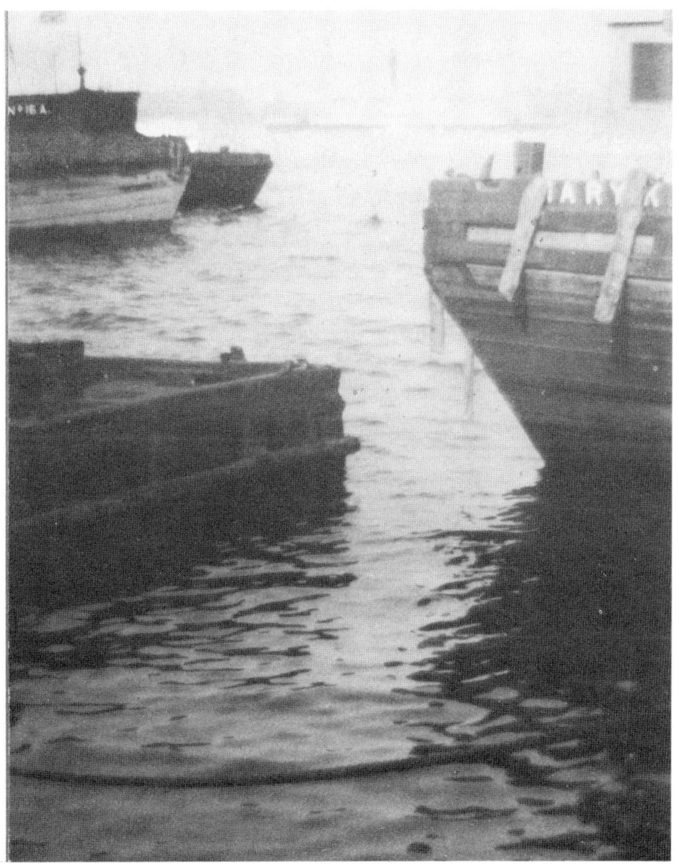

student of the noted photographer Clarence White and a "second-generation" member of the Photo-Secession. Stieglitz included the young photographer in the prestigious International Exhibition of Pictorial Photography at the Albright Art Gallery (Buffalo) in 1910 and, two years later, printed eight of his works in the April issue of *Camera Work*.[30] Many of Struss' photographs of New York (1909-1912) capture the form of the city, as well as the lives of the anonymous city people. Like Stieglitz's early work, these prints are, in spirit, "unusually close to paintings by the New York Realists (or Ash-Can School), sharing with them a structured approach to the casual flow of humanity."[31] *The White Ferry Boat* (Fig. 3), of 1909, reflects the city realist's interest in the rivers of New York. However, unlike the paintings of the Ash-Can School, subject matter is subordinated to formalistic concerns. That is, Struss is less interested with the image of the ferryboat, barely visible in the far distance, than with the balancing of abstract shapes and forms and the careful massing of lights and darks throughout the composition. This approach underscores the influence of Whistler and places *The White Ferry Boat* in the forefront of modernist tendencies in American photography.[32]

Though many associate the term Ash-Can School with scenes of street life, it is important to realize that the East River

Fig. 4 Everett Shinn. *New York Harbor*, c. 1898. Pastel on composition board, 7½ x 12⅜ in. Memphis Brooks Museum of Art; Memphis Park Commission Purchase 54.3.

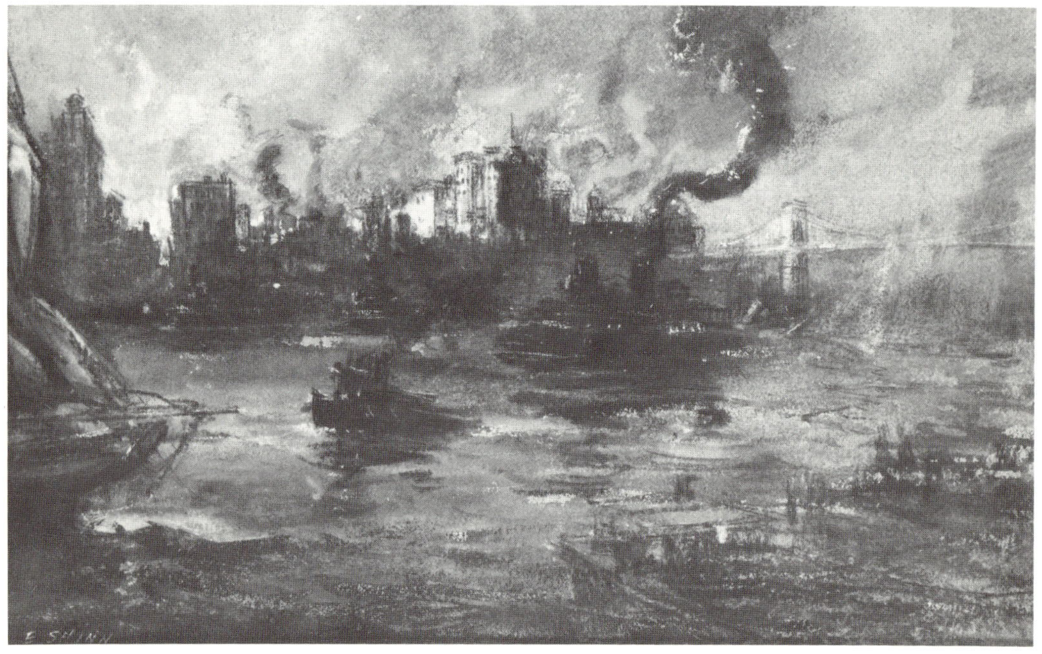

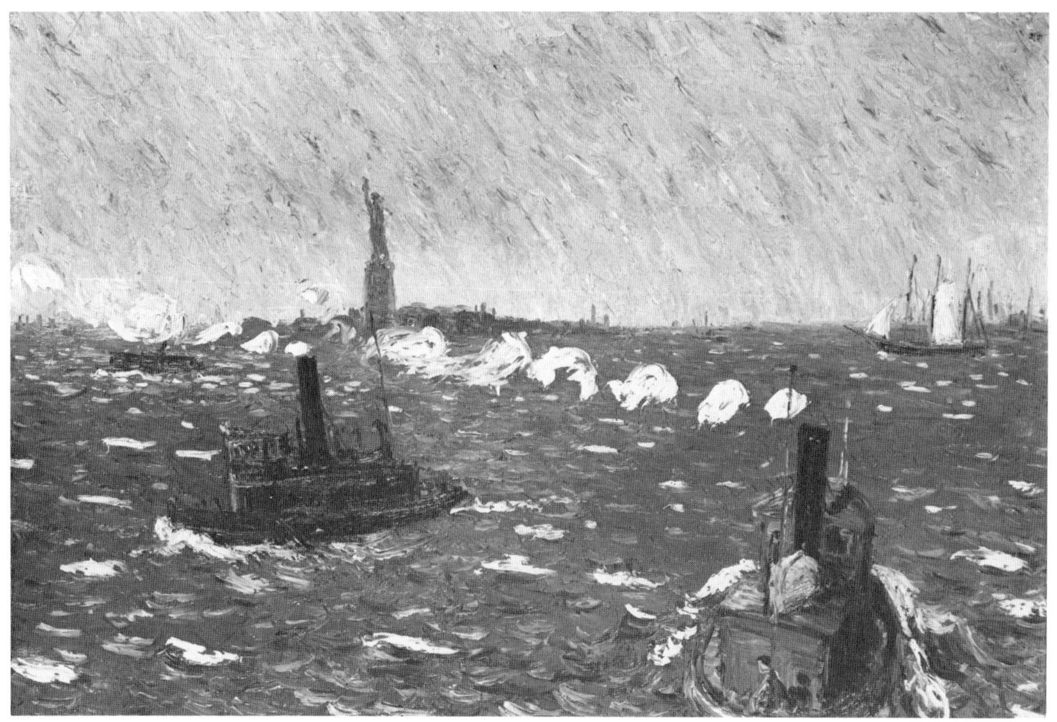

and the Hudson River provided rich and ample material for the city genre painters. They, more than the poets and photographers, captured the diversity of river life: youngsters frolicking in the river to escape the intense heat of summer; evening gatherings of the poor on the wharfs that border the rivers; and the drama of the river traffic from working tugboats to picturesque schooners traveling below the spectacular skyline of Manhattan (Fig. 4). The ferryboat provided yet another poetic interlude for the painters to observe and interpret. Whether rendered with the buoyant Impressionist palette of William Glackens (Fig. 5) or with the emphatic brushwork and broad tonal contrasts of Robert Henri (Fig. 6), one senses the river's vibrancy, immediacy, and dramatic quality that inspired and challenged the New York city realists.

Jerome Myers was one of the first artists to record the humble life of New York's Lower East Side. His work, as he has written, was "a simple song of the poor far from any annals of the rich . . . ."[33] Attracted to the vitality and color of the Italian and Jewish sections of New York, he rendered, with compassion and sympathy, the innocence of childhood and the poignancy of old age. He has been accurately called "the gentle poet of the slums."[34]

The ferryboat trips often provided unexpected adventures for the artist. Whitman, for example, noted the "queer scenes" that occurred: "children suddenly born in the waiting-houses" and masquerade parties "going over at night, with a band of music, dancing and whirling like mad on the broad deck . . . ."[35] Myers recounted a more harrowing experience:

> Once while sketching a young Italian mother and her baby on a Staten Island ferry boat, I was brought, violently and for the first time, face to face with an ancient superstition. Suddenly in the midst of my sketching, the young mother came at me like a tigress. 'You take my baby,' she screamed, 'I kill you!' The ferryman stood alongside me and between us we tried to pacify the frenzied woman. I tore up the sketch and threw the bits on the deck. Finally, the woman calmed down, and from her I gathered the explanation that her baby was not yet a year old and that therefore a picture of it would bring bad luck or worse. On that little trip I

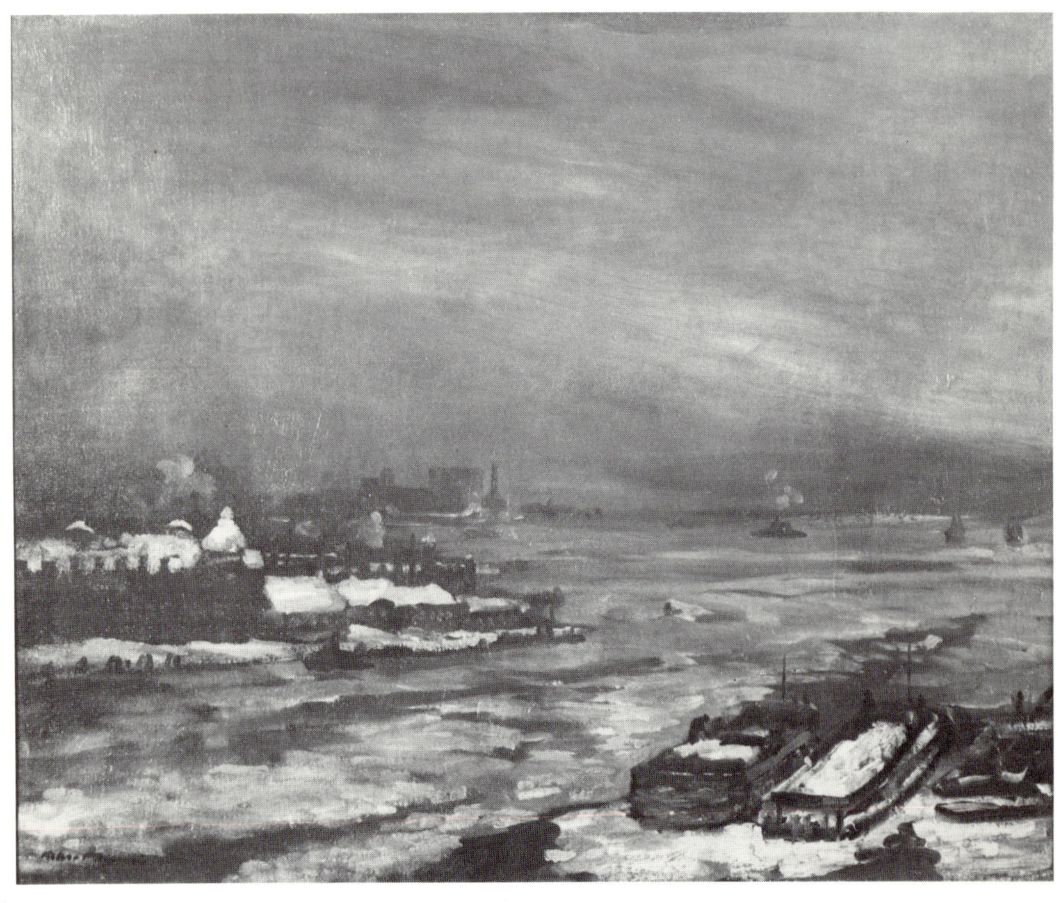

Fig. 6 Robert Henri. *East River, Snow*, 1900. Oil on canvas. 25¼ x 31½ in. The James A. and Mari Michener Collection; The Archer M. Huntington Art Gallery, The University of Texas at Austin.

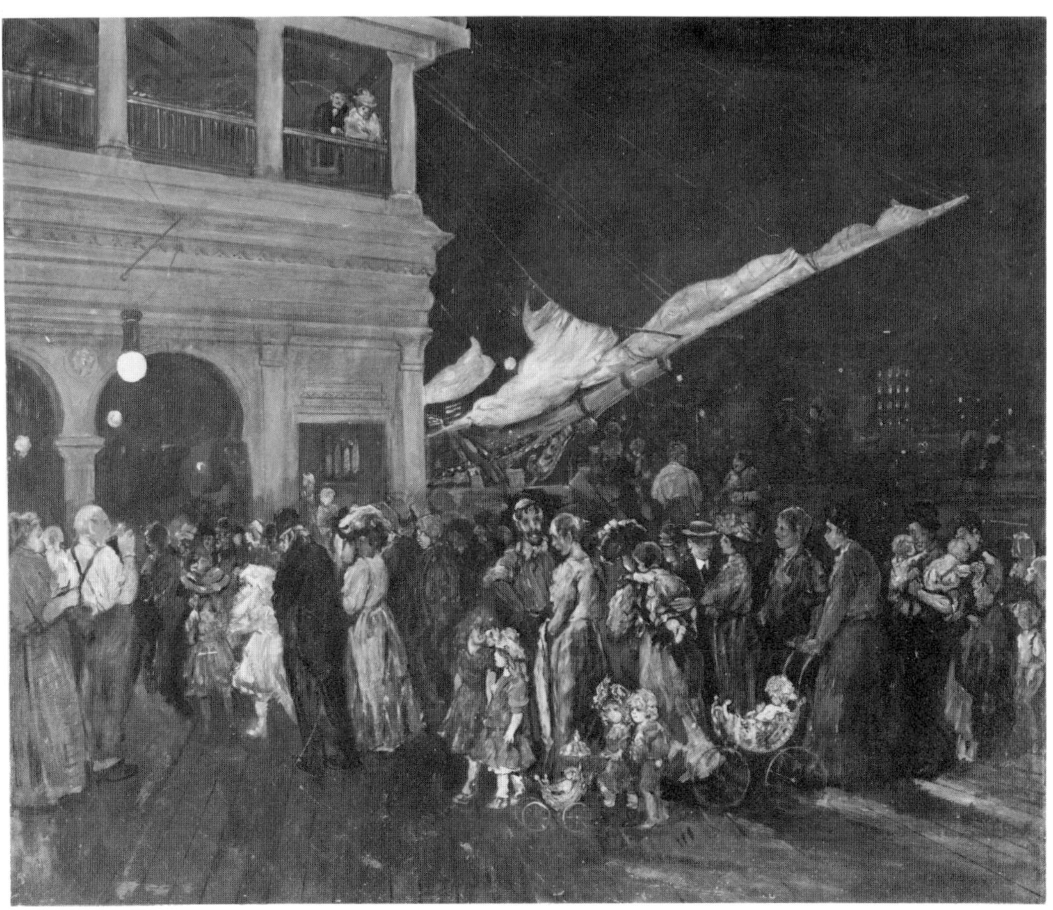

thus learned something to avoid, something which in all my experience, even in the Italian section of the city, I had never before encountered.[36]

Myers' 1905 painting, *At The Ferry Slip* (Fig. 7), records a more sanguine moment at the ferryboat and summarizes, in many ways, his artistic vision. Myers often painted working-class families enjoying their few hours together at evening concerts in the parks or on the recreational piers that border the rivers. The diverse ethnic types of the Lower East Side appealed to him, as did the children who joined their families for an evening ride on the ferryboat. These young boys and girls are invariably scrubbed and well-dressed, causing Sloan to remark that Myers always painted children in pinafores and pantaloons.[37]

Myers' (and the Ash-Can School's) interest in the work of Hals, Velasquez, Goya, and Manet is reflected in the muted palette and the loose brushwork. More important to Myers, however, was the legacy of Rembrandt. Of Dutch extraction himself, Myers wrote:

> It may be that Rembrandt's Dutch courage has sustained me, even as his art has inspired me. On faith and as an atavistic liberty, I have adopted him as an exemplar. I like to believe that had my difficulties been his, had he been exposed to the hectic contacts of New York, he would have acted much as I have.[38]

Both artists explored the ghettos of their respective cities and were able to evoke the sense of wonder they found in the humble lives around them.

Perhaps due to the circumstances surrounding his experience with the young Italian mother and her baby on the ferryboat, Myers usually painted the activity he found near the river's edge. *At the Ferry Slip* indicates that the artist remained on shore and intently observed the communal experience that the ferry provided for the immigrant families. Indeed, the wharfs and piers near the ferryboat house became stage sets upon which the lives of the urban poor were performed each summer evening: "Here whole families came for an evening outing. The men smoked and discussed politics. The women gossiped, the children played."[39] These daily events on the picturesque fringes of the river were a part of the city's rich panorama; they were also human documents that were both vital and pertinent to the artist.

Fig. 8 John Sloan. *Ferry Slip, Winter*, 1905-06. Oil on canvas, 21⅝ x 31¾ in. Hirshhorn Museum and Sculpture Garden, Smithsonian Institution.

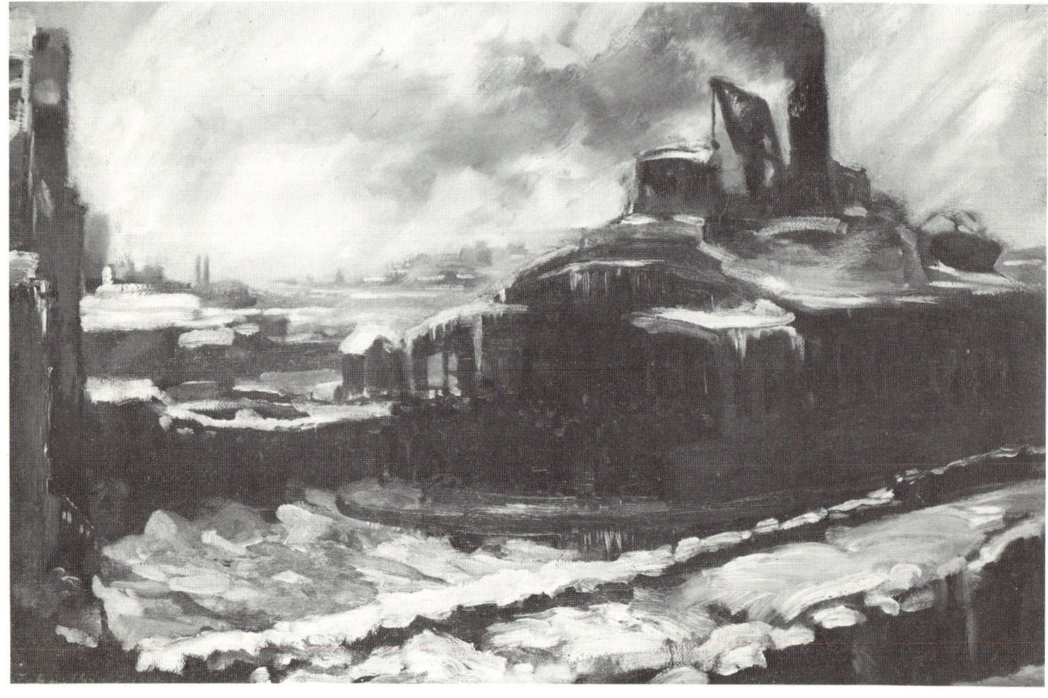

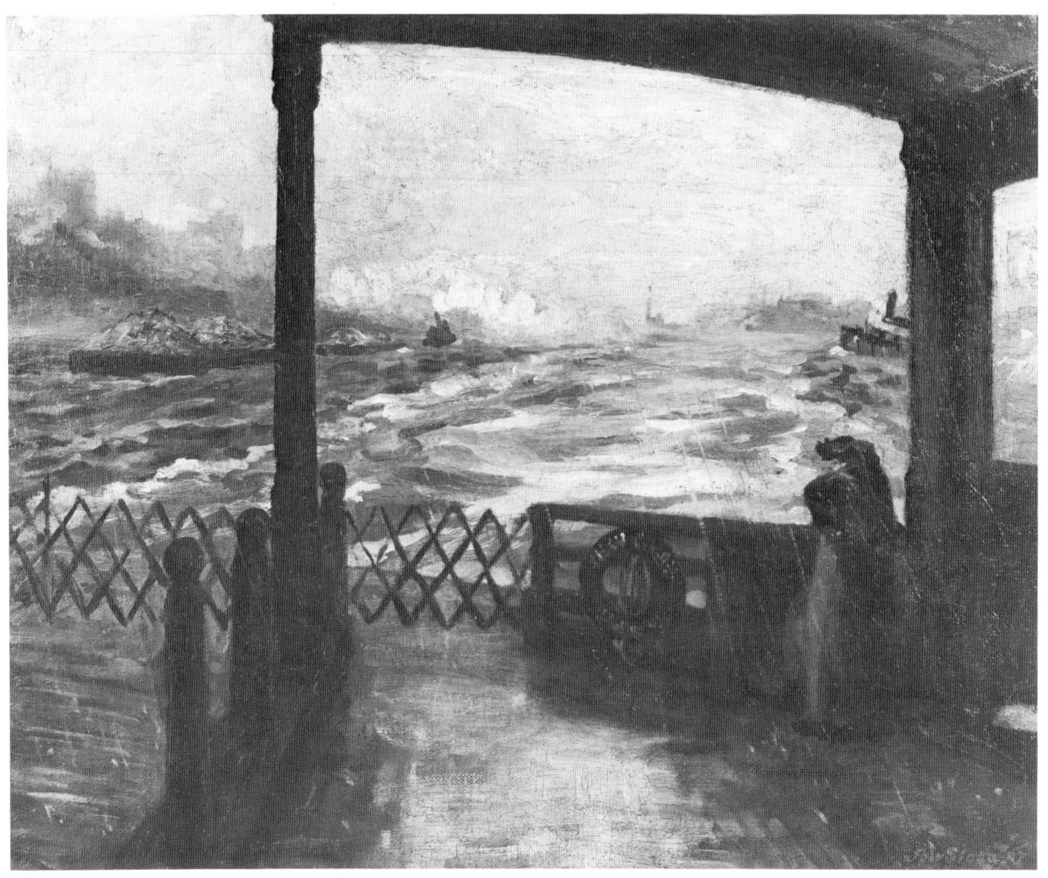

Fig. 9 John Sloan. *The Wake of the Ferry, I,* 1907. Oil on canvas, 26 x 32 in. Detroit Institute of Arts; Gift of Miss Amelia Elizabeth White.

Since the appearance of "Crossing Brooklyn Ferry" in 1865, the ferryboat has played a critical role in the interpretation of city life in American arts and letters. Whitman had predicted that "Fifty years hence others will see them as they cross." And many artists in the twentieth century did; none, perhaps, so brilliantly as John Sloan, a devotee of Whitman since the nineties. Standing on the Brooklyn Bridge for the first time, Sloan reflected on Whitman's poem and the crossing of the ferryboat. It is not surprising to discover that "Crossing Brooklyn Ferry" directly influenced Sloan's choice of the ferryboat as a suitable subject for the artist.

Sloan's first pictorial use of the ferry occurred in 1905 when he painted *Ferry Slip, Winter* (Fig. 8). A massive boat moves cautiously through the ice-packed Hudson River, "a non-impressionistic impression of an antique friend of the commuter fighting its way to berth against the mass of ice on a blustery winter afternoon."[40] The picture is a harmony of subdued color heightened by the reddish tones of the ferry. Detail is sacrificed to suggestion and form constructed with broad, emphatic brushwork. The boat itself, as one critic noted, is as imposing as a mountain by Courbet.[41]

Sloan returned to the theme of the ferryboat in 1907. On March 19, he wrote in his diary: "Went across the ferry to Jersey City. . . . Back from the ferry ride, I made a start on a canvas. 'The Wake of the Ferry' it might be called if it is ever finished."[42] *Wake of the Ferry, I* (Fig. 9) depicts a gray, melancholy day on the river. A single figure stands on the deck looking out at the frothy white wake created by the ferry. The somber tonalities of the sky, smoke, skyline, and water correspond in mood to the solitary loneliness of the woman. Sloan felt that this melancholic mood was "perhaps evoked by some nostalgic yearning for Philadelphia," as the ferryboat was "the first lap of the road home."[43] Finally, the composition, including the distant forms of the cityscape and the barges and tugboats on the river, visually echo several passages in Whitman's poem "Crossing Brooklyn Ferry:"

> The white wake left by the passage, the quick tremulour
> whirl of the wheels,

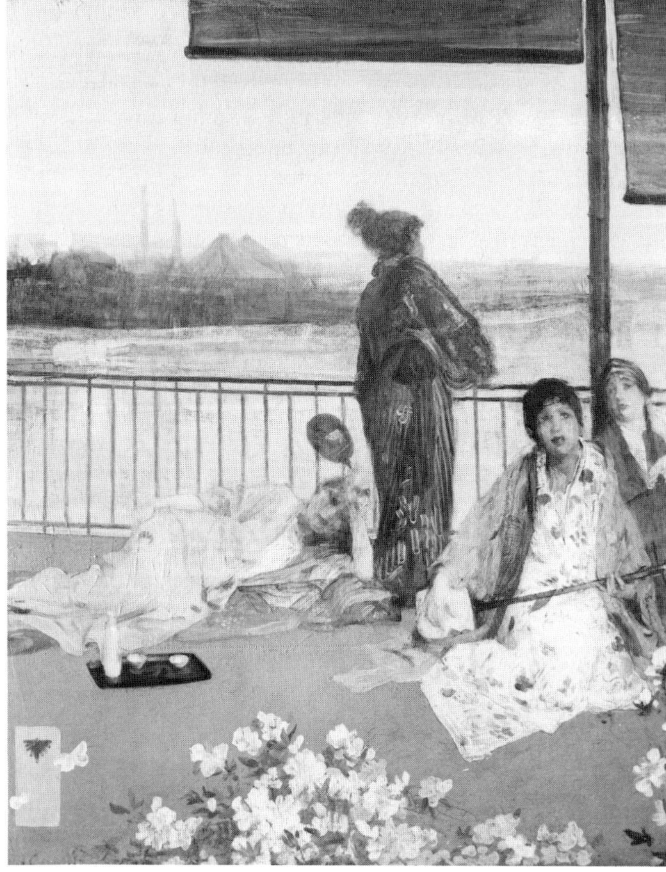

Fig. 10 James A. McNeill Whistler. *Variations in Flesh Color and Green: The Balcony,* 1868. Oil on wood panel; 24½ x 14¼ in. Freer Gallery of Art, Smithsonian Institution.

> The flags of all nations, the falling of them at sunset,
> The scallop-edged waves in the twilight, the ladled cups,
>   the frolicsome crests and glistening,
> The stretch afar growing dimmer and dimmer, the gray
>   walls of the granite storehouses by the docks,
> On the river the shadowy group, the big steam-tug
>   closely flank'd on each side by the barges, the hay-
>   boat, the belated lighter,
> On the neighboring shore the fires from the foundry
>   chimneys burning high and glaringly into the night,
> Casting their flicker of black contrasted with wild red
>   and yellow light over the tops of houses, and down in
>   to the clefts of streets.[44]

After working on the painting for approximately three weeks, Sloan apparently quarreled with his wife and "Threw a rocking chair through 'The Wake of the Ferry' . . . ."[45] The tone and date of the diary entry seem more reliable explanations for the damage to the painting than Sloan's later assertion that "The first one spurred by a rocking chair at a little party . . . ."[46] Though the painting "kicked around for 21 years"[47] before it was restored, Sloan remained enchanted with the theme and immediately began a second version of the picture.

Wake of the Ferry, II recalls the earlier canvas in mood and composition. Compositional modifications, however, were made. The posts of the ferry are handled with greater delicacy and suggest swaying movement by being placed at slight angles. Further adjustments are noted in the background. The mist-laden sky now casts a veil over the distant skyline, while the placement of several small boats plays a key part in the compositional balancing of the isolated figure. The form itself has undergone slight modification. Though the weight of the figure remains on the left foot, the stance and pose become more graceful and heighten the sense of movement in the second version. The change of color (from yellow ochre to red) in the pants also gives added visual weight to the introspective individual whose face is now entirely hidden from the viewer.

Sloan's simplification of realistic details and subtle harmonies of color and line in *Wake of the Ferry, II* reflect the pervasive influence of Whistler in American art at this time. In fact, Sloan's arrangement of the frame of an open deck, the lozenged-shape gate and the railing, the languid pose of the figure, the urban backdrop, and the delicate balancing of horizontals and verticals in a linear design specifically parallel formal elements found in Whistler's 1867 painting *Variations in Flesh Color and Green: The Balcony* (Fig. 10). Even the view of the ferry's upper deck corresponds in shape and placement to Whistler's use of a bamboo screen in his picture. It is important to remember that Sloan classified Whistler as one of his "gods" when he began to paint in the nineties. Perhaps more important

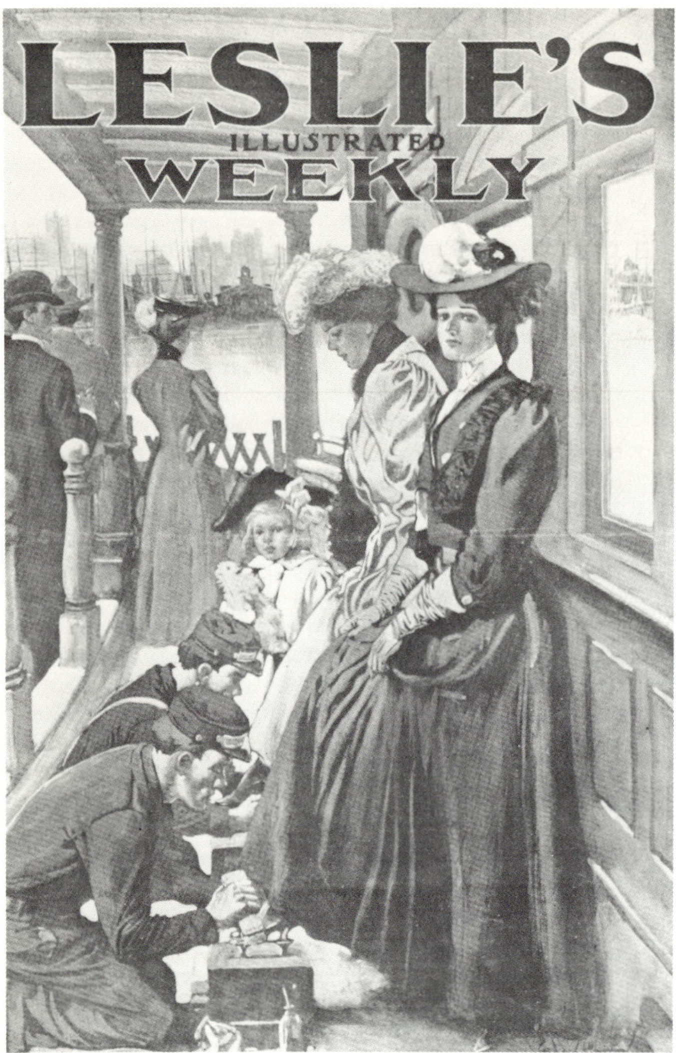

is the fact that Sloan had an opportunity to see *Variations in Flesh Color and Green: The Balcony* on exhibit in New York in 1903.

Though obvious stylistic relationships to Whistler are evident in both versions of *The Wake of the Ferry,* recent scholarship has explored the connection between the paintings of the Ash-Can School and late nineteenth-century magazine illustration. Images of urban life, commonly found in *Harper's Weekly, The Century Magazine, Scribner's Magazine* and other periodicals, anticipated by decades the subject matter of the city realist painters. As Richard S. Field has noted: "That the styles, subjects, techniques and public expectations of newspaper and magazine illustration influenced painting and drawing during the years around 1900 is hardly debatable."[48]

Fig. 11 G.W. Peters. "The Twentieth-Century Woman on a New York Ferry-Boat," 1907. *Leslie's Illustrated Weekly,* March 19, 1906.

Marianne Doezema, in an informative and provocative essay for the Cleveland Museum of Art, suggested that Sloan may have been inspired to paint *The Wake of the Ferry* after seeing an illustration that appeared on the March 19, 1906 cover of *Leslie's Illustrated Weekly* (Fig. 11). Entitled *The Twentieth-Century Woman on a New York Ferry Boat*, the illustration includes several elements present in Sloan's paintings: the wooden roof; the window at the right (in *Wake of the Ferry, I*); and the railing on the back of the ferryboat. Doezema concluded that "the approach to the subject and motivation for creating a realistic image that is a record of life was related to the approach and motivation of an illustrator."[49] Whether or not Sloan was directly inspired by G. W. Peter's illustration in *Leslie's Illustrated*, his work as an illustrator for newspapers and magazines in Philadelphia and New York supports Doezema's contention that he was familiar with popular illustrations of city life in America. It also provides another interesting link to Walt Whitman in that both painter and poet were aware of, and artistically profited from, the tradition of world art and the world of popular culture.

The many direct and indirect connections between Whitman and Sloan raise the question as to whether the figure in *The Wake of the Ferry* refers, however obliquely, to the "good gray poet." The 1855 engraving of Whitman by Samuel Hollyer (Fig. 12), copied from a lost photograph taken a year earlier by Gabriel Harrison, appeared in the first edition of *Leaves of Grass*. A contemporary description of the Whitman portrait reveals several characteristics reminiscent of Sloan's figure: "represented in a garb, half sailor's, half workingman's, . . . 'wideawake' perched jauntily on his head, one hand in his pocket and the other on his hip. . . ."[50] By reversing the figure, Sloan replaced the poet's "expression of pensive insolence" with the painter's expression of introspection. The conclusion that the Hollyer engraving was in Sloan's mind when he painted the picture cannot be substantiated by any comment the artist ever made. Perhaps the figure is merely an intriguing visual rhyme of the Whitman portrait, as the painting itself is a visual counterpart of many passages in "Crossing Brooklyn Ferry."

The Wake of the Ferry, II was first exhibited at the Folsom Galleries in 1912. From that time to the present, the melancholy mood evoked by the isolated figure has claimed the attention of the majority of critics. One 1912 review stated:

> At first glance it is an empty canvas and then slowly it fills with the life of the one figure in the shadow. You cannot escape entering into her thoughts, into the sorrows that have come to her. And the chances are that you recall someday when you too, stood desolate, looking out over the receding waters, wondering too, of your future.[51]

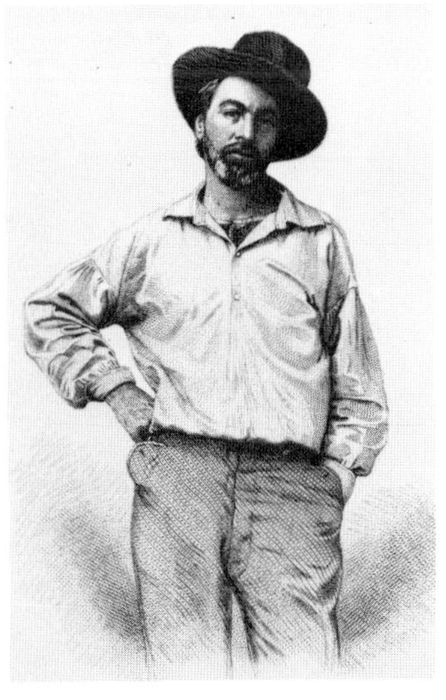

Fig. 12 Samuel Hollyer. *Portrait of Walt Whitman*, 1855. Engraving (after a photograph by Gabriel Harrison, 1854), The Huntington Library, San Marino, California.

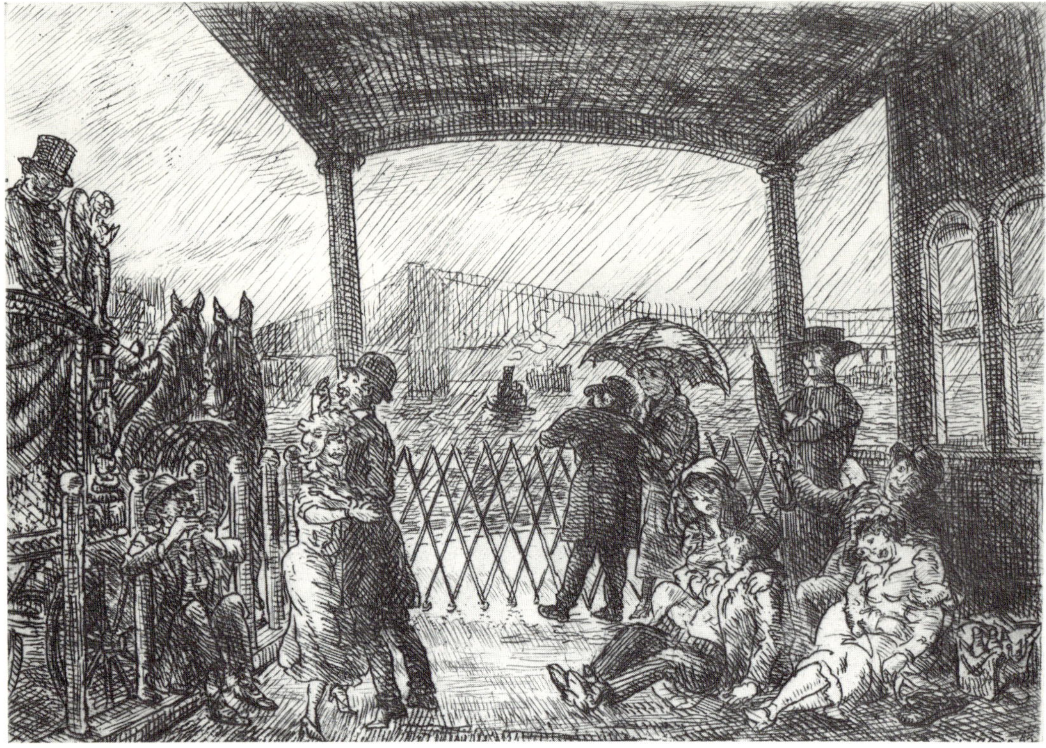

In 1937, Lewis Mumford wrote:

> When in the 'Wake of the Ferry,' Sloan shows a lonely
> figure of a woman, standing partly exposed to the rain,
> looking out over the gray waters, he symbolizes forever
> the intense loneliness, as final as that of a deserted hermit
> on a Himalayan peak, almost everyone has known in the
> midst of crowded Manhattan.[52]

Approximately half a century later, Mumford reiterated his love
for that "great turtlelike creature," the ferryboat, and his
admiration for *The Wake of the Ferry, II*, concluding that "no
painter has come back with a picture comparable to John
Sloan's 'Ferryboat Ride' . . . ."[53]

Two final episodes in the history of the painting are worth
noting. In 1949, the Cleveland Print Club asked Sloan to make
an etching for its membership. Their letter to Helen Farr Sloan
praised several of Sloan's early city etchings and then asked
"Would he care to repeat any of these subjects or do something
similar in the lithographic medium? Would he be interested in
making a print similar to some of his paintings, such as the
glorious Wake of the Ferry? "[54] Naturally, Sloan was perturbed
by requests asking him to repeat work done forty years earlier.
Yet he responded with characteristic humor: "I won't do it.
But that gives me an idea for a humorous plate, 'The Wake on

Fig. 13 John Sloan. *The Wake on the Ferry,* 1949. Etching, 5 x 7 in. (plate). Private collection.

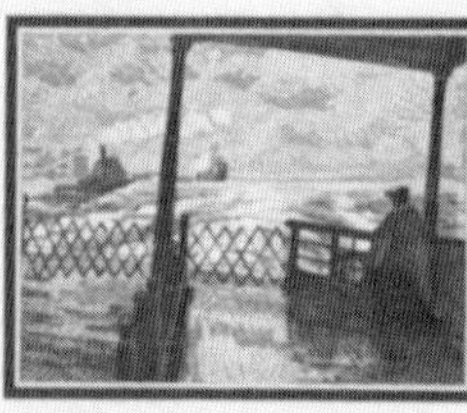

Fig. 14 Bradbury Thompson. John Sloan Commemorative Stamp, 1971. United States Postal Service.

the Ferry' (Drunken Irish 'Wake')."[55] Sloan drew the initial tissue sketch in Santa Fe on August 21, 1949. The following day the images of "A hearse and merry-making mourners on the front of a ferry boat"[56] were transferred to a copper plate which went through four states before satisfying the artist (Fig. 13).[57] Three-hundred and fifty proofs were printed (one hundred by Will Shuster in Santa Fe and two-hundred and fifty by Ernest Roth in New York), an unusually large edition for Sloan. None were sent to Cleveland, but two hundred were given to the Art Students League in New York for sale to the League members. *The Wake on the Ferry*, a parody of his 1907 masterpiece, was the last etching Sloan ever made.

Finally, a national tribute to Sloan and *The Wake of the Ferry* occurred in 1971 when the United States Postal Service selected the painting to represent the artist's achievement in art. Designed by Bradbury Thompson, the eight-cent commemorative stamp (Fig. 14) was issued on August 2, 1971 in honor of the 100th anniversary of Sloan's birth.

John Butler Yeats referred to John Sloan as a painter of dream pictures. Most people, whether critics, connoisseurs, or laymen, would place *The Wake of the Ferry, II* within that Yeatsian category. The deep humanity that pervades the picture and gives it universal significance epitomizes the spirit of Sloan and the New York Realists. "In every work of true art," Yeats wrote, "there is always a final result, a something, a magic, an incantation, a music, which sweetens and releases the spirit."[58] To view *The Wake of the Ferry, II* is to discover this extraordinary quality in art.

Notes

1 The term "Ash-Can" first appeared in 1916 and "Ash-Can School" was introduced into art historical literature by Holger Cahill and Alfred H. Barr, Jr. in *Art in America in Modern Times* (New York, 1934), p. 31. For a brief history of the term, see William I. Homer, *Robert Henri and His Circle* (Ithaca and London, 1969), pp. 280-281. "The Eight," another name associated with the city realist painters, refers to a group of eight artists (Robert Henri, John Sloan, William Glackens, Everett Shinn, George Luks, Maurice Prendergast, Ernest Lawson, and Arthur B. Davies) who exhibited at the Macbeth Gallery in New York City in February, 1908. The exhibition was a direct challenge to the restrictive exhibition policies and conservative attitudes of the National Academy of Design. A landmark in the history of American art, the exhibition helped set the stage for other important exhibitions, including the 1910 Exhibition of Independent Artists and the 1913 Armory Show.

2 Guy Pène du Bois, *Artists Say the Silliest Things* (New York, 1940), p. 82.

3 John Sloan, *John Sloan's New York Scene: From the Diaries, Notes and Correspondence 1906-1913*, ed., Bruce St. John (New York, 1965), p. 395.

4 Milton W. Brown, *American Painting from the Armory Show to the Depression* (Princeton, 1955), p.13.

5 Walt Whitman quoted in Paul Zweig, *Walt Whitman: The Making of the Poet* (New York, 1984), p. 214.

6 John Collier, *A Manual of Oil Painting* (London, 1886), p. 39. Sloan, however, rejected other ideas advocated by the author. Collier wrote: "For the painter who can live amongst the common people, and can thoroughly enter into their lives and habits, there is the possibility of most interesting pictures." (*Ibid.*, p. 40) Conversely, Sloan felt that "It is not necessary to go out and 'have experiences' to understand and imagine the feelings of others." (John Sloan, Unpublished Notes, 1950; John Sloan Trust)

7 George Moore, *Modern Painting* (London and New York, n.d.), pp. 213-214.

8 Robert Henri, "The New York Exhibition of Independent Artists," *Craftsman*, XVIII (May, 1910), p. 161.

9 David W. Scott, *John Sloan* (New York, 1975), p. 35. Also see Bruce St. John, "John Sloan in Philadelphia, 1888-1904, *"The American Art Journal,* III (Fall, 1971), pp. 80-87.

10 Lloyd Goodrich, *John Sloan* (New York, 1952), p. 17.

11 Walt Whitman, "Pictures," in *Leaves of Grass,* "Comprehensive Reader's Edition," eds., Harold W. Blodgett and Sculley Bradley, *The Collected Writings of Walt Whitman* (New York, 1965), p. 645.

12 Sloan, *New York Scene,* p. 40.

13 *Ibid.,* p. 133.

14 Mary Fanton Roberts, "John Sloan: His Art and Its Inspiration," *Touchstone,* IV (February, 1919), p. 362.

15 John Butler Yeats, "A Painter of Pictures," *Freeman,* IV (January 4, 1922), p. 402.

16 See Roger B. Stein, *Seascape and the American Imagination* (New York, 1975) and John Wilmerding, *A History of American Marine Painting* (Salem and Boston, 1968). Also see Gerald Eager, "The Iconography of the Boat in 19th-Century American Painting," *College Art Journal,* XXXV (Spring, 1976), pp. 224-230.

17 Lewis Mumford, *Sketches from Life: The Autobiography of Lewis Mumford, The Early Years* (Boston, 1982), pp. 126-127.

18 Zweig, *Whitman,* p. 108.

19 Though Emerson's famous letter of 1855 heralding this "most extraordinary piece of wit and wisdom that America has yet contributed" and Whitman's anonymous laudatory reviews have become part of the Whitmanic legend, the general reception to the publication of *Leaves of Grass* was "All in all . . . close to being a non-event." (See Zweig, Whitman, pp. 219-220.)

20 Van Wyck Brooks, *Howells: His Life and World* (New York, 1959), pps. 193-194.

21 William Dean Howells, *The World of Chance* (New York, 1893), p. 12.

22 William Carlos Williams, "The Wanderer," in *The Collected Earlier Poems of William Carlos Williams* (New York, 1951), p. 3.

23 Williams, "Pastoral," in *The Collected Earlier Poems. . . . .,* p. 124.

24 Stieglitz founded the Photo-Secession in 1902 on the principle that photography was a fine art. His struggle against the "fetters of

conventionalism, tradition and provincialism" that dominated photography in America (Alfred Stieglitz, "The Photo-Secession," in *American Annual of Photography and Photographic Time Almanac* [New York, 1904], p. 42) paralleled the city realist's confrontation with the doctrines of the National Academy of Design.

25 Alfred Stieglitz quoted in Dorothy Norman, *Alfred Stieglitz; An American Seer* (New York, 1973), p. 39.

26 Zweig, *Whitman*, p. 214.

27 J. Nilsen Laurvik, "Alfred Stieglitz, Pictorial Photographer," *International Studio*, 44 (August, 1911), xxv. Quoted in Homer, *Alfred Stieglitz and the Photo-Secession* (Boston, 1983), p. 19.

28 William I. Homer, *Alfred Stieglitz and the American Avant-Garde* (Boston, 1977), p. 20.

29 Homer, *Alfred Stieglitz and the Photo-Secession,* p. 19.

30 Founded by Stieglitz in 1903, *Camera Work* grew out of the Photo-Secessionist movement and became one of the leading disseminators of modern ideas in American arts and letters.

31 Homer, *Alfred Stieglitz and the Photo-Secession,* p. 151.

32 The Struss Pictorial Lens, designed by the photographer in 1909 and manufactured in 1915, may have been used to create *The White Ferry Boat*. The lens apparently enabled Struss to render a delicate line and "an unusual quality of light, texture, depth, reality, and richness of tone." Karl Struss, *Pictured with the Struss Pictorial Lens* (New York, 1915), p. 2.

33 Jerome Myers, Unpublished Manuscript, Jerome Myers Papers, Delaware Art Museum.

34 Lloyd Goodrich and John I.H. Baur, *American Art of our Century* (New York, 1961), p. 27.

35 Walt Whitman, *Specimen Days* (Boston, 1971), p. 82.

36 Jerome Myers, *Artist in Manhattan* (New York, 1940), pp. 55-56.

37 Grant Holcomb III, *The Life and Art of Jerome Myers* (Unpublished Master's thesis, University of Delaware, 1971), p. 60.

38 Myers, *Artist in Manhattan*, p. 75.

39 *Ibid.*, p. 231.

40 John Sloan, *Gist of Art* (New York, 1939), p. 206.

41 Walter Pach, *L'Art et les Artistes,* XVIII (February, 1914), p. 224.

42 Sloan, *New York Scene*, p. 113.

43 Sloan, *Gist of Art*, p. 209.

44 Whitman, "Crossing Brooklyn Ferry," in Walt Whitman, *Complete Poetry and Uncollected Prose* (New York, 1982), pp. 309-310.

45 Sloan, *New York Scene,* p. 119.

46 Sloan, Unpublished Notes, John Sloan Trust.

47 John Sloan, File Card, John Sloan Archives, Delaware Art Museum.

48 Richard S. Field, *American Prints 1900-1950* (New Haven, 1983), p. 14. Also see Emily Bardack Kies, *The City and the Machine: Urban and Industrial Illustration in America 1800-1900* (Unpublished dissertation, Columbia University), and *City Life Illustrated 1890-1940: Sloan, Glackens, Shinn — Their Friends and Followers* (Wilmington, Delaware, 1980).

49 Marianne Doezema, *American Realism and the Industrial Age* (Cleveland, 1980), p. 57.

50 Quoted in Emory Holloway and Ralph Adimari, *New York Dissected* (New York, 1936), p. 154.

51 "Art Notes: American Life by American Painters," *Craftsman,* XXIII (December, 1912), p. 371.

52 Lewis Mumford, "The Art Galleries: The Life of the City," *New Yorker* (February 27, 1937), p. 32.

53 Mumford, *Sketches from Life,* p. 126.

54 Cleveland Print Club to Helen Farr Sloan, July 13, 1949. John Sloan Trust.

55 John Sloan, Unpublished Diary, July 15, 1949. John Sloan Trust.

56 *Ibid.*, August 21, 1949.

57 See Peter Morse, John Sloan's Prints: *A Catalogue Raisonnè of the Etchings, Lithographs, and Posters* (New Haven and London, 1969), pp. 348-349.

58 John Butler Yeats, "The Work of John Sloan," *Harper's Weekly* (November 22, 1913), p. 20.

List of Works in the Exhibition

JOHN SLOAN (1871-1951)

Ferry Slip, Winter, 1905-06
Oil on canvas, 21⅝ x 31¾ in.
The Hirshhorn Museum and Sculpture Garden,
Smithsonian Institution, Washington, D.C.

The Wake of the Ferry, II, 1907
Oil on canvas, 26 x 32 in.
The Phillips Collection, Washington, D.C.

The Wake on the Ferry, 1949
Etching, 5 x 7 in. (plate)
Private collection.

WILLIAM J. GLACKENS (1870-1938)

Breezy Day, Tugboats, New York Harbor, c. 1910
Oil on canvas, 26 x 31¾ in.
The Milwaukee Art Museum; Gift of Mr. and
Mrs. Donald B. Abert and Mrs. Barbara Abert
Tooman.

JEROME MYERS (1867-1940)

At the Ferry Slip, 1905
Oil on canvas, 25¼ x 30½ in.
The Metropolitan Museum of Art; The George
A. Hearn Fund, 1966.

EVERETT SHINN (1876-1953)

New York Harbor, c. 1898
Pastel on composition board, 7½ x 12⅜ in.
Memphis Brooks Museum of Art; Memphis
Park Commission Purchase 54.3.

ALFRED STIEGLITZ (1864-1946)

The Ferry Boat, 1910
Photogravure, 8⅛ x 6½ in.
Stephen White Gallery,
Beverly Hills, California.

KARL STRUSS (1886-1981)

The White Ferry Boat, 1909
Platinum print, 4¾ x 3¾ in.
Stephen White Gallery,
Beverly Hills, California.

ROBERT HENRI (1865-1929)

East River, Snow, 1900
Oil on canvas, 25¼ x 31½ in.
The James A. and Mari Michener Collection;
The Archer M. Huntington Art Gallery,
The University of Texas at Austin.

Designed by Mary Farris
Printed by Commercial Press
Production by L. Ortiz Art Service
Copyright© 1984 by the Timken Art Gallery
and Grant Holcomb